Is Your L♥ve Tank Full?

Is Your Love Tank Full?

or, Are You Loving on Empty?

DENNIS SWANBERG

Our purpose at Howard Publishing is to:

- *Increase faith* in the hearts of growing Christians
- *Inspire holiness* in the lives of believers
- *Instill hope* in the hearts of struggling people everywhere

Because He's coming again!

Published by Howard Publishing Co., Inc.,
3117 North 7th Street, West Monroe, LA 71291-2227

99 00 01 02 03 04 05 06 07 08   10 9 8 7 6 5 4 3 2 1

Edited by Philis Boultinghouse
Interior Design by LinDee Loveland

Library of Congress Cataloging-in-Publication Data
Swanberg, Dennis, 1953–
Is your love tank full? or, Are you loving on empty? / Dennis Swanberg.
p. cm.
ISBN 1-58229-001-6
1. Spouses—Religious life. 2. Marriage—Religious aspects—Christianity.
3. Bible. N.T. Corinthians, 1st, XIII—Criticism, interpretation, etc. I. Title.
BV4596.M3S93 1998
242'.644—dc21   98-20177
CIP

Contents

to my wife,

Lauree,

who always keeps the Swan's love tank full

Introduction

Times sure have changed, haven't they? When I was a kid, my sweet little mama, Pauline Bernadeen, wouldn't have dreamed of having her own car. She was quite content to borrow Daddy's (Floyd Leon) car on Saturday to grocery shop and run errands. Now, most families have at least two cars; many even have extras for the teenagers.

My wife, Lauree, can't imagine waiting until Saturday to do all that she has to do. Now I gotta tell you about my Lauree. She's my honey love. She's my little Lauree, four foot eleven and goin' to heaven. And she has the "hottest" invention in family cars since the station wagon—the *Suburban*. It's the kind that holds forty or more people—the kind that makes the Middle East sheiks cheer when you put your foot to the gas pedal, because as soon as you start moving, that gas disappears.

Well, the cost of gas has changed too. When I was back in high school, I could pull up to the pump and say, "Give me a dollar's worth, please." Then off I'd drive, knowing I could run around with my buddies for most of the night. If I went up to the pump today and put a dollar's worth in, I'd be lucky if I got out of the parking lot. I mean, you almost have to take out a small loan to fill that thing up!

Since I've started traveling more, the responsibility of taking care of the Suburban has fallen on Lauree's petite little shoulders. Now when I'm on the road, I think about Lauree a lot. She's a good-looking woman. When I see her I go,

"Hubba, hubba" (sort of an unknown tongue). But I don't think too much about all that she has to juggle back home.

There have been many times when I've come home from a trip that I've wanted to take my family out to eat or to a movie. We'd all jump in the car—all excited and ready to go—and then we'd discover that the gas gauge was on "E." I don't mean just the orange part of the "E," I mean way down past the warning zone. Well, on one such occasion, I rocketed into a little tirade, "Honey, you need to fill up this car! You know you shouldn't let it get below a quarter tank. What would happen if you ran out of gas, got stranded, and I was out of town? What would you do? Good night, woman, you've got to think about those things."

And then my honey love let me in on the real picture. "Honey," she said with all the sweetness she could muster, "while you're on the road, having a good time, I'm here at home working hard to do it all!" And being the bright guy that I am, I immediately started back-pedaling, "Okay, baby, you are so right." And if you guys out there are smart, you'll know when it's time to step back and say, "Okay, baby; you're right."

So now when I come home from a trip, one of the first things I do is check the gas gauge. If it's below a quarter of a tank, I go fill it up. No questions asked! I just take a good book or a newspaper and sit back and get comfortable while the numbers on that digital display tick away.

When I get home, I immediately find Lauree so I can be sure she knows what I've done for her. "Hey, baby, look! I filled up our chariot. I did it just for you." And Lauree is so impressed. She says, "Thank you, honey, that helps me so much." And then I get to say, "Yeah, baby!"

You see, when that gas tank is full, we're all happy. Lauree can go to the mall, run her errands, and take Chad and Dusty where they need to go. Life is rich and full of promises when

I've made sure that Lauree's gas tank is full. It's that same feeling I had back in high school when I would say, "Fill 'er up." I felt like the world was mine for the taking! And now, when I know Lauree's gas tank is full, I feel confident that I have taken care of her. I know she can put gas in her car by herself. She's not helpless; it just makes me feel good to do it for her.

And as husbands and wives, we all have *love tanks* that need to be constantly replenished. And sometimes that can be fairly costly—sometimes we have to make sacrifices, and sometimes we have to give up a bit of our precious time. But the end result is well worth the effort.

Conflicts in marriage are created when couples unknowingly fail to make each other happy or when they deliberately hurt each other—in other words, when they don't fill up each other's love tanks. You see, I didn't fill up the Suburban's gas tank because I didn't realize it was empty. Some husbands may not take care of their wives' cars because they don't think it's their responsibility. Our *love* tanks fail to get filled up for the same reasons.

Keeping your honey's love tank full requires diligent effort. But sometimes, we offer excuses instead. First, there's the *I didn't know* excuse. This is where the husband or wife "innocently" shrugs their shoulders and says, "Duh, I had no idea there was a problem." Then there's the *It's not my job!* excuse. Here the spouse insists that if the other partner needs "filling," they can do it themselves!

However—I say—*however,* that's not the biblical idea of love. Throughout this book, we're going to look at the teachings about love found in 1 Corinthians 13. And we're going to see that if we want our marriage to run smoothly, we have to be proactive in our love—we have to put some fuel in our baby's love tank. We can't plead ignorance, and we can't shuffle the responsibility.

Ol' Swan may not know much, but I've come to realize that a car's performance is in direct relation to what I put into the tank—garbage in, garbage out. And the same is true for your lovin' spouse. If you put bad fuel into your honey's tank, you will not have a smooth-running marriage. We seem to understand this principle when it comes to our children. We know that what we put into them has a direct bearing on what they grow up to be. And so, we expose our children to healthy, Christian activities and people. We go to great pains, and sometimes great expense, to see that they get a good education and to see that they are surrounded by good friends and loving adults. Well, the same concept applies to our marriage relationships.

So, buckle your seat belts and get ready to join the caravan of folks learning how to keep their marriage love tanks full. This journey has blessed thousands of couples already, and you can be part of the fun. Whether you've been married for a few months or many years, by the time you get to the last chapter, you and your mate will be cruising along on the super highway of love and you, too, will be able to say, "Yeah, baby!"

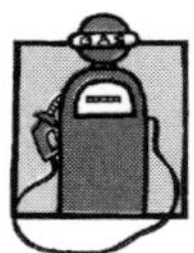

Fill up on the Word—1 Corinthians 13

The beautiful "Love Chapter," written by the apostle Paul, tells us all we need to know about how to love the people in our families. Too many people make the mistake of applying these verses to how they love everyone but their families, but our homes should be the first place we live out these beautiful characteristics. Throughout our journey together, we'll be making regular pit stops in 1 Corinthians 13 to fill up on God's Word about loving our families.

CHAPTER ONE

HUMOR

A cheerful heart is good medicine, but a crushed spirit dries up the bones.

Proverbs 17:22

Things turn out
best for the people who make
the best of the way things
turn out.

Art Linkletter

You grow up the day you have your first real laugh—**at yourself.**

—Ethel Barrymore

Laughter is the **shortest** distance between two people.

—Victor Borge

Laughter is a tranquilizer with no side effects.

—Arnold H. Glasow

Don't Squeeze the Charmin

I love to laugh, and I love to make other people laugh. But I've discovered in my travels across the country that an inordinate number of church folks are afflicted with *sour-puss-itis*—the disheartening disease that manifests itself in furrowed frowns and stiff arms folded across chests. It's almost as if those folks think, "If I'm not suffering, I'm not doing this Christian thing right. I'd better not *ever* look like I'm having fun."

Well, I couldn't disagree more.

humor

A big part of my ministry is making people laugh. When I deliver messages to groups across the country, I intentionally add humor to my presentations, and one of my favorite kinds of humor is impersonations. I've found that one of the best cures for sour-puss-itis is to break out in the voices of some of our all-time favorite characters like Barney Fife, Jimmy Stewart, or Billy Graham. When I'm speaking, these characters are likely to show up anywhere that has been infected by the deadly sour-puss-itis.

The other night I had a vision featuring one of my favorite characters. Did you know that eating Mexican food after 9:00 P.M. can cause you to have visions you know not of? Well, it can. And on this particular night, I sat straight up in bed at 3:00 A.M. with a salsa-inspired vision of Jonah. Now you may not know this, but Jonah is a distant ancestor of Forrest Gump. And in my vision Jonah stood and said, "This is my testimony: I was running from God, and I got in my Bubba Gump shrimp boat and sailed away as fast as I could. But a big storm came up, and I fell overboard. I surely would have drowned were it not for the giant fish that swallowed me up. I stayed in that stinky belly for three days and three nights, and then that giant fish spit me out on shore, sort of bit me on the buttocks. God told me to preach to the Ninevites, so that's what I finally did. And that's all I'm going to say about that. Stupid is as stupid does."

Some of the best humor comes from taking an on-the-spot situation and finding the laughter in it. Now you need to know that I got my preacher training from Southwestern Baptist Theological Seminary. In that seminary, I learned how to preach! I knew when to be loud and forceful, and I knew when to talk soft and low. I even knew how to cry when the occasion required, like during a building campaign. Once, as a young, overly confident preacher—

right out of seminary—I was preaching for a little country church. And I was feeling pretty good about myself.

I'd developed the habit of making my grand entrance right behind the choir. Being the last one out made quite an impressive entry. Well, on this particular Sunday I had to visit the "little room" before services started. This little country church had only *one* little room—it was "coed" before that word was popular. Not only was it little, it was right next to the choir room, and it didn't have any insulation. No insulation meant the choir *knew* I was in the little room, and I knew the choir was in the choir room. As I was completing my little-room tasks, I heard the choir leaving. Could they not wait on me? Didn't they know how important it was that I bring up the rear of their procession?

So I hurried as fast as I could and hooked up with them just in time—just as the last ones were entering the sanctuary. I made my grand entrance—all calm, cool, and collected—and marched right up on the platform. But when I turned to face the audience, I noticed several people poking each other in the ribs, pointing at me, and giggling behind their hands. Within seconds the whole group had broken into full laughter. Well, I didn't know what to think.

I checked my zipper—but it was up and in the locked position. I finally looked down and saw that a six-foot piece of toilet paper had stuck to my shoe in my haste to catch up with the thoughtless choir. Well, what do you do in a situation like that? You turn it into laughter. I just took hold of that toilet paper and wrapped it around my leg. The little old ladies in the back were just dying laughing. I almost entitled that message, "Don't squeeze the Charmin." What a great service we had that morning!

People laughed when they didn't expect to laugh. They started their day in laughter and continued it in joy. While there surely are times when you need to be serious, don't fall into the trap of taking yourself too seriously. In fact, the Bible reminds us in Proverbs 17:22 that "a cheerful heart is good medicine." That toilet paper wrapped around my foot probably did more good than the Geritol those ladies took that morning!

Healthy relationships include laughter. Every relationship, whether it is with your spouse or your children, can be filled with joy. Laughter puts a spark in your relationships and keeps your everyday routines from creating boring ruts in your life. Because you invest humor in your relationships does not mean they lack emotional depth. In fact, the opposite is true. Humor adds new and intense emotions to your relationship. Sometimes an aversion to laughter may be a cover-up for some deep-seated fear. Being able to laugh at yourself and at situations that aren't supposed to be funny are signs of emotional security and emotional good health.

I guess that makes ol' Swan one of the most secure and healthy guys around. Because I love to laugh, I love to make Lauree and Chad and Dusty laugh. Laughter is one of the fuels that keeps my relationships going. Our homes don't have to be tombs of drudgery and gloom. Instead, they should overflow with laughter and joy. If you want your children to come home for holidays and reunions, make it a place worth coming home to. Make it a happy place to live and then a happy place to visit. You don't have to be a stand-up comedian to accomplish this task. Just create a climate and circumstance where laughter becomes a part of your daily life.

You've heard the saying, "Life is what you make it." That means we have a choice. We can choose to have a life full of frustration and fear, but we can just as easily choose one of joy and contentment.

Show your family that it's okay—no, it's better than okay—it's essential to laugh. Fill up your family's love tank with a generous supply of laughter.

FILL UP ON THE WORD—1 CORINTHIANS 13

Pride and anger are enemies of humor, and Paul addresses both of these menaces in the Love Chapter. "Love is . . . *not proud* . . . it is *not easily angered.*" One of the basic ingredients of a healthy sense of humor is the ability to laugh at yourself. When we're puffed up with pride, we don't laugh at ourselves; rather we get angry and huffy when things go wrong. If you want people to feel comfortable around you, to enjoy being with you, then learn to laugh at yourself and find humor in life's little mishaps. Laughter oils the squeeky parts of life and keeps your engine hummin'.

Check Your Gauge

1. How do you react when you make a silly mistake—like tripping over the carpet or saying something *really* stupid. Do you get defensive and huffy, or do you laugh?
2. When was the last time your family had a good laugh together? What did you laugh about? How did it affect the atmosphere in your home?
3. What's the difference in laughing at your own mistakes and making fun of someone else's? Why is one okay and the other not?
4. How does laughter benefit you?

humor

Ready, Set, Go!

Make a conscious effort this week to bring laughter and joy into your home. Set a goal to bring a smile to the lips of everyone in your home at least once a day.

CHAPTER TWO

GIFT-GIVING

It is more blessed to give

than to receive.

Acts 20:35

It is not how many years we live, but what we do with them. It is not what we receive, but what we give to others.

Evangeline Booth

It is more blessed to give than to receive. And besides, you don't **clutter up your attic.**

—Franklin P. Jones

The world is full of two kinds of people, the givers and the takers. The takers **eat well**—but the givers **sleep well.**

—*Modern Maturity*

The Deer Stand Has Carpet

"Brother Dennis, I just don't know what's the matter with that wife of mine!"

This "good ol' boy" deacon wanted me to help him understand his wife. But I was thinking, I can't even understand my own wife; how am I gonna help him understand his? But when a deacon calls, a minister responds. So, he came to my office and continued his lament. "I just can't figure that woman out. She's always saying how I never buy her gifts, so I went out and bought her the nicest gift I could think of. I got her a deer stand, second to none. Cost me seven hundred forty-nine dollars. Why, I put a heater in there and some carpet—I even put in her own adjustable seat—but she's only used that deer stand one time! I just don't know what else to do."

So I began to explain—as gentle as I knew how—that most women spell deer stand H-y-a-t-t, or some version thereof. A wise man learns to give his wife gifts that have meaning to her. While the deer stand may have seemed the perfect gift to this deer-hunting deacon, it wasn't exactly what his dainty wife had in mind. Learning how to give meaningful gifts to your spouse is one way to keep your love tank full.

Take Lauree for instance. She loves to buy gifts. Why, I'm convinced she goes up to perfect strangers and asks if there's anything she can buy them. To her, gift-giving is a way to express love. And she's good at it. I mean, she always seems to choose the perfect gift. You know, the kind that always brings exclamations of, "That's *just* what I wanted!"

Oh, how I longed to hear those words one Christmas a few years ago. All of my family had come to spend Christmas Eve with us for the traditional opening of presents. I had thought long and hard about what to give Lauree that year, and I waited anxiously as she opened my first gift to her—a beautiful set of golf clubs. I was so proud of those golf clubs and just knew she would be too. But her only response was a tight-lipped, "Thank you very much." I may not be a real bright guy, but I could tell right away that the gift I thought was a sure thing was a complete strikeout. But there were two more gifts to go, so there was still hope.

I was pretty confident about gift number two because it was something *girlie*—you know, one of those sheer, dainty, little nighties designed by someone named Frederick. My eyes were wide open and my ears alert, anxiously awaiting words of praise for a husband who could really pick a gift. Instead, all I got for my efforts was another polite "thanks." My dad piped in with his usual words of wisdom, "Try again, next year, son," and Lauree just rolled her eyes. But wait, I had one more chance.

Lauree unwrapped gift number three with much hesitation. I'm sure she was wondering what odd object was waiting for her in that box. But when she unwrapped the gift, I heard a string of melodious "ooh's" and "ahh's"—the like you've never heard. It was one of those Dooney Burke, or Gooney Durke, little purses. I could breathe again! I had finally hit on a gift that she wanted. You see, the golf clubs were my subtle way of trying to get her interested in playing golf. The nightie, well, there's no need to explain why I gave that gift. But the purse was for her, not for me. That year I learned the hard way the importance of choosing a gift that *she* really likes.

Now, whenever I need to get my honey love a gift, I make a beeline for her favorite stomping ground, the mall. I head straight for a store called Petite Sophisticate (it's that store for little people, 'cause she's so little). I walk in, hand them her picture and her measurements, and say, "I want the most expensive thing you have in here." I have them wrap it up, and I head for home. When I get home I say, "Hey, baby, I looked all over the mall to find you the perfect gift." And she loves me for it!

The great thing about gift-giving is that there are all kinds of gifts you can give that don't cost you a dime! But the principle remains the same: Give gifts that mean something to the other person, not that necessarily mean something to you. Find out what kind of compliments lift your spouse. Does he like to hear what a handsome he-man he is, or does mentioning his kind actions mean more? Does she like to hear what a good mom she is, or would she rather you tell her how great she looks? There's definitely more than one correct way to compliment your spouse. But the point is, find out what winds your spouse's clock and wind it *their* way, not yours.

You can also give little gifts of kindness and thoughtfulness throughout the day. But think first: What does my spouse consider kind and thoughtful? What means something to you may not be all that meaningful to your mate. Make the effort to find out! That's the key.

God is the ultimate gift-giver. He is the supreme example. He's given us what we so desperately need, things that no one else can give. His gifts to us are salvation, mercy, grace, hope, and so much more. His gifts are free to anyone who wants them, aren't they? God's gifts are not tricks to get us to give him something; rather his gifts flow out of his loving nature. God desires what is best for us. This is exactly how we should be with our spouses. Our gifts should never be out of selfish desire for what we will receive in return. They should never be tricks or bribes to insure behaviors we want to see in our spouses.

Ephesians 4:32 says, "Be kind and compassionate to one another, forgiving each other, just as in Christ God forgave you." Forgiveness is one of the most precious gifts of all—especially when it comes to family relationships. Husbands and wives hurt each other almost every day—in little and big ways. If forgiveness is given freely and often, your love tank will overflow with love. And there are countless other free gifts you could give your spouse. How about the gift of patience or honesty or respect?

I'm convinced that if you shower your spouse with a few of these gifts, then sprinkle in a few thoughtful trips to the mall, your love tank will be full.

Fill up on the Word—1 Corinthians 13

I think it's fair to say that *"love rejoices in the truth"* can be applied to the art of gift-giving. When you care enough to learn the truth about what matters to your spouse, when you seek to understand his or her needs, you are well on your way to becoming a expert gift-giver. Paul also tells us that love *"does not boast."* So as you practice your newfound skill of gift-giving, be careful to keep your attitude free of pride and boasting. Give, not for the praise it will bring, not to satisfy your ego, but give because your heavenly Father has taught you how to give by giving the most precious gift of all and by giving it with no thought to what he will get in return.

CHECK YOUR GAUGE

1. What was the last gift you gave to your spouse? Why did you give it?
2. What traits of gift-giving can you learn from God as you develop your gift of giving?
3. Why is it so important to know what your spouse wants and not just give gifts that you would appreciate?
4. How can gift-giving be prideful? What characteristics should it have instead of pride and boasting?

Ready, Set, Go!

Set aside some time with your spouse to talk about the kinds of gifts you like. Talk about more than just material gifts. Express appreciation for past gifts that were especially meaningful.

3

CHAPTER THREE

Honor

HONOR

A

Be devoted to one another in brotherly love. Honor one another above yourselves.

Romans 12:10

Three keys to more abundant living: caring about others, daring for others, sharing with others.

William A. Ward

By the time we realize our parents may have been **right**, we usually have children who think we're wrong.

—*Bits and Pieces*

Everybody needs a **hug.** It changes your metabolism.

—Leo Buscaglia

Hug Your Mama

I love my mama—my little Pauline Bernadeen. When I was growing up, my mama had certain standards she tried to impose on me, and one of them was proper attire. There was many a morning when I would leave for school and she would block my path and proclaim, "You have nicer things to wear than what you have on. I would be ashamed, absolutely ashamed of what you have on."

I'd say, "But, Mama, this is what all the kids wear."

"I don't care what they wear. It hurts,

you know. It really hurts. Your daddy and I work so hard. It hurts me, and it hurts your daddy."

I'd say, "He don't look hurt."

"He's hurt. Believe me, he's hurt. I wonder what those teachers think of your mama. What you wear is a reflection on me, you know."

And then when I'd come home from school, my little mama would be there waitin' for me. Mama is a hugger, and when I came home from school, she wanted a hug. "Hug your mother," she'd say. But one particular afternoon, I just didn't feel like a hug.

"Ah, Mama, I don't want to hug."

But I'd chosen the wrong day to protest, 'cause my daddy, Floyd Leon, was in the living room sitting in his Lazy Boy recliner. "Hug your mother, son," he said.

"I don't want to hug," I insisted.

"I said, *hug your mother.*"

About this time, Mama started getting all upset. Have you ever noticed that when mamas get upset, they kinda double up on the syllables. "So-on, I ju-ust want a little hu-ug."

Now this really got to Daddy, and he was bound and determined that I was gonna hug my mama. Like I said, he was sitting in his Lazy Boy recliner, and he grabbed that lever and brought that chair down with a boom. Next thing you know, I had my arms around my mama—but just barely.

"That's not a hug," she protested.

I looked over at my daddy, and I could read his lips, and he said, "Hug your mother," real slow and determined like.

So I picked her up, squeezed her tight, kissed her right on the mouth—like in the movies—and set her back down.

"I am your *mother,*" she exclaimed, "your *mother.* I don't care for *that* kind of hugging and kissing."

"But isn't that the way you and daddy kiss?"

Well, now that I've grown up just a little, I

understand the value of hugging my mama, and I also understand the importance of honoring those your love.

I learned a valuable lesson about how good a little special effort can make you feel while I was away at college at Baylor University. You know, going off to college and leaving the comforts of home is not easy. I have to admit I really missed my mama. I was in Waco, Texas, and my mama was in Austin. I might as well have been on the moon.

The pastor in Waco, at the time, Marshall Edwards (my father in the ministry), had lived in Austin when I was growing up. And he had been my high school football chaplain (we called him "Rabbi"). He and his good wife, Doris, invited several of the students over to their house for a meal. To say we were excited would be putting it mildly. We were ecstatic! The thought of a home-cooked meal got our mouths to watering and our imaginations going. We gathered at their house one Friday evening, eager for some good home cookin'. Doris announced that dinner was about to be served, but said she wanted to ask us each a question before we ate. She started with my friend Allen.

"Allen," she said,"what's your favorite meat dish?" Puzzled, he answered, "Meat loaf." I'm thinking I'd never really gotten into meat loaf because growing up, our meat loaf had so many crackers in it I'm not really sure you could call it *meat loaf.* Anyway, she looked at Allen and said, "Well, I have made your favorite meat dish. I've made meat loaf." She then went from student to student, each time asking what their favorite food was and then declaring she had made it for them. Soon it was my turn. "Dennis, what is your favorite dish of all dishes?" she asked.

I knew she wouldn't have this dish. I had never told anybody what my favorite dish was. I didn't even think my mama knew. So I said, "You won't have this one."

"Try me," she said.

"Okay," I said doubtfully, "It's creamed peas."

And do you know what Doris said? She said, "I made creamed peas just for you."

"You made creamed peas!" I exclaimed. "How did you know?"

Doris went on to explain that she had called all our mamas. *She'd called our mamas.* Can you imagine how we felt when we realized she cared enough about us to find out a seemingly insignificant detail about each one of us. A detail that made us feel as if we were the most important people in the world. You gotta love it! You gotta love it when someone puts time and energy into making others feel special.

That day I felt like I was in a giant arena and someone had called my name out while crowds of people cheered me on. Doris had taken some of her valuable time to make phone calls, shop, and then prepare several different dishes. Oh, what a valuable lesson on bestowing honor I learned that day. This gracious woman taught me how much I love feeling honored and special. Everyone does.

We all have the need to feel like we are "super special" to someone. It's a fuel very few of us can do without. And one of the best ways to honor a loved one is to express admiration for who they are and what they do. Dr. Willard J. Harley lists the need for admiration as one of the ten most important emotional needs. But it's been proven that the need for admiration is stronger in the male population. We just love it when our wives brag on us or cook us a special meal. In fact, we thrive on it. I'm convinced that a major component in any man's success is a supportive wife standing beside him, cheering him on.

Now, don't get me wrong. Just because I said men need it more than women doesn't mean that women don't need it too. They do! A well-placed compliment like, "Lauree, those are about the best tasting creamed peas I believe I ever did eat," can make Lauree feel like a queen. Just like I want her to feel.

If you guys don't make your wives feel like queens and you wives don't make your husbands feel like kings, you've got some repentin' to do! God calls us to make the love of our lives feel special. A good way to start is to compliment your spouse on a job they have done. Husbands, tell your wife what a good job she does balancing all her many different roles or tell her how nice she looks in her new dress. Wives, brag on the job your husband does at the office or how well he relates to his children. Thank him for putting his family first and for being a spiritual leader. But be honest in your admiration. Look for the things your spouse does right, brag on them, and you'll be surprised at how your compliments will shape his or her behavior in the future.

Another way you can show honor, recognition, and love to your spouse is to go the extra mile. Try to think of something you can do to make your spouse feel really special. Be sneaky, like Doris, and surprise your spouse with something unexpected. When you do that, your effort will say, "I love and admire you so much that I took some extra time out of my day to see what matters to you."

Do you want to know the sad thing about the story of our special meal with Doris? You know, it hurt me when I realized it. My mama knows what my favorite dish is, but I don't know what hers is! I think I'll give Pauline Bernadeen a call. She's bound to need a "fill up."

HONOR

Fill up on the Word—1 Corinthians 13

In 1 Corinthians 13, Paul reminds us that love "does *not envy* . . . it is *not rude* . . . it *keeps no record of wrongs.*" In addition to telling us what love is, Paul also tells us what love is not. And if we want to bestow honor on our spouse, we will refrain from all of the above. Envy will eat away at love about as fast as anything. When we honor our spouses, we are happy for their successes. There is no room for envying the good in their lives. Rudeness is an attitude that can creep into a marriage little by little until all courtesy and kindness is gone. We're usually much more aware of common courtesies with people outside our home, but somehow, when we walk in that front door, we leave our manners behind. Kindness and courtesy go a long way toward filling your spouse's love tank.

And finally, if we truly honor our loved ones, we will keep no record of wrong. It's easy to harbor little grievances in our heart against our mates. But the problem with little grievances is that they grow up. If something's really bothering you, discuss it with your spouse; otherwise, let it go—keep no record of wrong.

CHECK YOUR GAUGE

1. What lessons about honor did you learn from your childhood? Are you living what you learned today?
2. When was the last time you did something special and unexpected for your spouse? What kind of reaction did you get?

HONOR

3. What compliments can you pay your spouse today? If you need a little time to think of one, take the time!

Ready, Set, Go!

Every day for a whole week give your spouse at least one genuine compliment. Notice what this does for your spouse. Put some mental energy into dreaming up something extra special and unexpected that would bring honor to your mate, and do it this week.

4 CHAPTER FOUR

INSPIRATION

Encourage one another

daily, as long as it is

called Today, so that none

of you may be hardened

by sin's deceitfulness.

Hebrews 3:13

I was going around in a circle until Jesus gave me a compass.

To make your dream come true, you have to—**stay awake.**

A friend is someone who can **see through you** and still enjoys the show.

Whatever your lot in life, **build** something on it.

—Readers Digest

You Make Me Want to Be a Better Man

In September of 1997, the whole world grieved the death of Mother Teresa. She never had much, she never wanted much, but she had a heart that overflowed with the love of Christ. She saw people others never saw. She saw needs no one else took the time to see. She hurt for those who hurt. She cried with those who cried. She showed the world how to love the unlovable. And she inspired others to capture her vision and to respond with a love inspired by a frail, old woman in faraway Calcutta.

Who inspires you? Who helps you capture a vision of how you can impact the world? Who inspires you to tackle the difficult? Who challenges you to follow your impossible dream?

Jack Nicholson and Helen Hunt starred in a movie about two people trying to develop a "meaningful" relationship. Nicholson's character is a gruff, noncommunicative man, and Hunt's character is a single mother dealing with a sick child. She is tired and doesn't want to play games with this relationship. At one point, she says to him, "Stop right now and give me a compliment." So he gives her that famous Nicholson look and slowly, purposefully says, "You make me want to be a better man."

Wow! What a line! I pray that there is someone in your life who makes you want to be a better man or woman. I also pray that you are that person in your spouse's life, that you are the one who inspires him or her to be a better person, to dream dreams, to climb mountains, to overcome insurmountable obstacles. At the 1998 Oscars, one of the winners said that her win was proof that dreams do come true. Do dreams really come true? Not always. But when they do, there is usually a list of people to thank who helped make those dreams a reality—just like at the Oscars—lists so long they now have to limit the response time.

How will your spouse's dreams ever become a reality if you don't encourage those dreams? Would your name be on the thank-you list when those dreams are realized? You see, everything in our world of reality says, "Dreams don't come true. Just get back to work. One person can't change anything." But most people don't know the power of inspiration.

You may have heard the story of the mediocre high school football player who showed up to play a game on the day after his blind father died. Everyone was surprised to see him at the game. He explained to the crowd that while his dad had *listened* to every game he had ever played, this would be the first game his father would actually *see*. Or perhaps you heard the story of the runner whose father saw him collapse on the track and came out of the stands and carried him across the finish line. Stories about parents who inspire their children to greater heights excite and challenge us.

But our children are not the only ones who need our inspiration. Our life-mates need it too. We should be the ones to say, "What is your dream? How can I help you attain it?" Sadly, far too often the husband is not supportive of his wife's dreams. Maybe she wants to go back to school or start a business. But her husband only offers a list of why it cannot be done. Maybe his own insecurities keep him from wanting her to succeed. And how many husbands have been worn down by a wife who, instead of cheering her husband on, continually whines, complains, and ridicules?

When the world does not believe in you, you can still keep going. But when the one closest to you does not believe in you, defeat will follow. When I began the life of a pastor, I needed Lauree to believe in me. I knew my mama believed in me, and that was important. I knew God believed in me, and that was very important. But I needed Lauree to believe in me too. My love for her and my boys and their love for me inspire me to be a better man. I want to be a better person for them and for God. That is an unstoppable combination—a desire to please God and to please those you love on earth.

The mental pictures we hold of ourselves shape our actions, feelings, and behaviors. Sometimes those pictures are distorted and false, but we still act as if they are true. If we believe we are weak, we will act as if we are weak. If we believe we are strong, we'll act as if we're strong.

Start now to inspire your mate to want to be a better person. Help your spouse see him- or herself as a success, as one who can accomplish great things. Inspire your mate to actions, feelings, and behavior that is God sent and God centered.

Be generous with the "fuel of inspiration." It is one of the most powerful and effective tools we have for helping others grow. Fill your spouse's love tank with it till it overflows.

Fill Up on the Word—1 Corinthians 13

"Love *does not delight in evil* but *rejoices with the truth*. It always *protects*." If we are to be the "wind beneath our spouse's wings," as Bette Midler so beautifully sang, we will look for the positive in our mates, not the negative. We will rejoice in their successes, not gloat in their failures. It's easy to point out the "evil" in our husband or wife; it's easy to remind them of past failures when they dare to share new dreams. But love *rejoices in the truth* of their dreams and even goes the extra mile to *protect* their fragile dreams by offering encouragment and inspiration, by expressing confidence and support. What a blessing to be able to inspire another person to become more of what God intended him or her to be.

Check Your Gauge

1. What are your spouse's dreams?
2. What are you doing to encourage or discourage those dreams?

3. If you have trouble supporting your mate's dreams, why? Look inside yourself for the answer, not at your mate's shortcomings.
4. If you've not encouraged your mate in the past, what can you do now to inspire your spouse to fulfill his or her dreams?

Ready, Set, Go!

If you don't know what your spouse's dreams are, ask him or her. Then ask what you can do to help fulfill those dreams. If you already know what your life-mate dreams about doing, verbally express your support and offer whatever help you can to help fulfill those dreams.

5

CHAPTER FIVE

SHARING TIME

Sharing Time

Be very careful how you live. Do not live like those who are not wise, but live wisely. Use every chance you have for doing good, because these are evil times.

Ephesians 5:15–16 NCV

Time is the glue
that bonds a broken heart,
but love is the air which
dries the glue.

Don't let yesterday use up too much of **today**.

Today is the tommorow we worried about yesterday.

A **stitch in time** saves embarrassing exposure.

Sucrets and Tonis

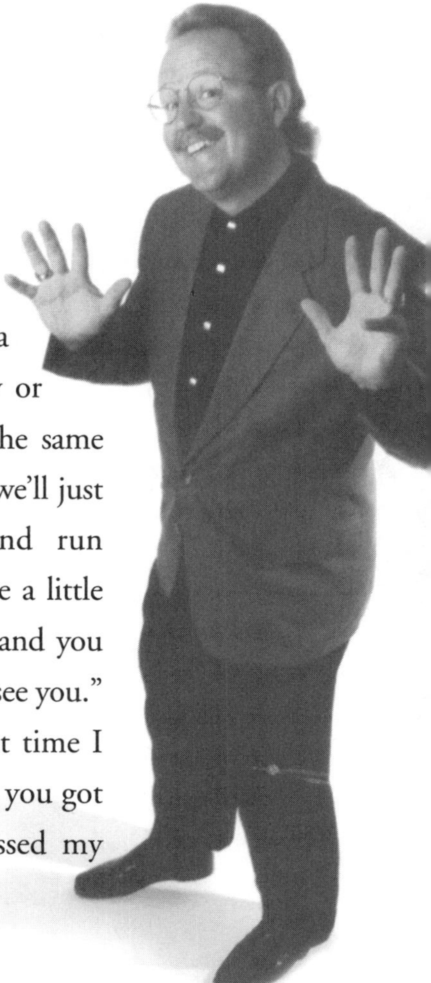

Whenever I ask my mama what she wants for her birthday or for Christmas, she always says the same thing: "I want *you*. For one day, we'll just be *together*. We can shop and run errands—just like when you were a little boy. And I'll get my hair done, and you can watch. Wanda would love to see you."

"Oh, Mama," I say. "The last time I went with you to Wanda's place, you got one of those Tonis, and it messed my allergies up for weeks."

Do you remember those Toni perms? They used those pink little spongy rollers and those little squares of paper. I remember watching the lady fix Mama's hair with bobby pins from the Sucret box. I didn't know what a Sucret was until I was at Baylor University. I was walking down the athletic dorm hall one night, and I happened to glance in this room. I saw a guy put something in his mouth from a Sucret box. I didn't even know the guy, but I rushed into his room and said, "Man, don't put that in your mouth!" He asked me what he was supposed to do with it. I told him, "Put it in your hair!"

Anyway, when I was a kid, my mama liked nothing better than to haul me around town to keep her company. That's still her wish today. Back in my teen years, there was a song that said time keeps on slipping, slipping into the future. My mama knows the value of time and has lived long enough now to know how quickly it slips away. Our present is too soon our past, and our future too soon our present. Think about that once in a while. Do you remember how when you were young, it seemed an eternity from one Christmas to the next? Now as an adult, you don't get your bills paid from one Christmas before the next is here. Time truly does slip away.

That's why Mama wants to be with me. Reality says that she won't be here forever, and neither will I. Loving someone means investing time in that person; it means building a relationship. Isn't it true that anything worthwhile requires time investment? Doesn't the amount of time we spend on something greatly affect what it becomes? And doesn't the time you spend on something reflect its value to you? Time spent reflects your level of commitment. And this is especially true of the time we spend with our life-mates.

Too often, when the honeymoon is over, we tend to slack off on the effort we expend. We think, "We're married now. I don't have to invest the kind of time I did while we were dating. I've got him (or her) now." While we may "have" him or her, it takes time investment and hard work to "keep" the marriage strong and growing.

We have to *work* at finding ways to spend time together. The everyday family activities can be overwhelming. We're all involved in so many. Children may be involved in band, football, tennis, gymnastics, basketball, karate, and more. They go to the movies, play video games, and go to birthday parties. Men have responsibilities at work, at church, and at home. They attend conferences, seminars, and ball games. And they may even work in a round of golf or two. Women juggle work, school, tennis, church, children, and hobbies. The lists are endless. We have all become so busy that even our "breaks" are now subject to a ticking clock. Meals have become fast food, typewriters have become computers, country roads have become superhighways—all in an effort to give us more time, and now we don't have time for anything.

Before fast food, computers, and superhighways, we had time to sit and talk, time to plant a garden, and time to cook a pot roast. Relationships were developed over the fence or on the front porch with a tall glass of lemonade. Couples took walks in the evening, and families attended church revivals that lasted a week. It kind of makes you wonder where all that time is going that we are saving. I certainly have trouble finding it, and I'm sure you do also.

But we can't go back in time. Our world has changed for better and for worse. It's our responsibility to "redeem the time" and make the best choices we can. The truth is that everyone has the same twenty-four hours in a day and several lists of activities to choose from. How we choose to use our time is the challenge. Setting priorities is crucial.

I want to know that I make Lauree's list, and I want her to know she makes mine. In fact, after God, our spouses should be the next most important thing on our lists. How do we make sure that happens? Well, I don't believe it can happen with the new "quality time" versus "quantity time" theory. I'm not so sure all my trips to town with Mama were *quality* time, they were just time spent being together. There's not much quality in a beauty shop of gossiping ladies. But that didn't matter. We were together. We have to be careful that we don't buy into this new philosophy and try to "schedule" a relationship like we schedule a hair appointment.

What really builds relationships is *time spent together*, lots of time. You and your spouse going to church together, watching your children play ball, picking out a new car, having the family over for dinner, going to the mall, grocery shopping—these everyday activities, done together, are the building blocks of a good relationship.

Observing a spouse or a parent doing the right thing will do more to draw you closer to that person than any conversation about doing the right thing. And to observe, you have to be there. You have to spend time with your mate and your children.

Time is one of the most expensive and one of the least expensive fuels that you can put in your husband or wife's love tank. Its price is greater than all the money in the world. The price is *you.* You are your most valuable commodity. Fill your spouse's love tank with undiluted, premium *you.*

Fill up on the Word—1 Corinthians 13

"Love is *patient* . . . it always *perseveres*." I don't know about you, but I can be quite selfish with my time. There's only so much of it, and I have so many things to fill it with. That's why these two phrases from 1 Corinthians 13 are so important as we seek to invest time in the ones we love most. It takes *perseverance* to deliberately set aside time for people. Jobs and responsibilities outside the family compete loudly for our time. But we must persevere and follow through with our commitments to the most important people in our lives.

And spending time with some people—perhaps especially our children (or our mama while she gets a Toni)—requires a good bit of patience.

We could get things done so much faster and more efficiently! And sometimes the activities others want us to be involved in seem a waste of time, and we grow impatient. But you can't put a price tag on the value of time invested in the ones you love. Patient, loving, caring time together reaps *eternal* dividends. I'd say that's a wise investment.

CHECK YOUR GAUGE

1. What does your spouse like you to spend time with him or her doing?
2. When was the last time you did the activity you named above?
3. What seemingly insignificant (but truly meaningful) ways do you and your mate spend time together?

4. When your husband or wife spends time with you doing what you like, how does that make you feel?
5. What competes for your time with your mate? What changes can you make to have more time together?

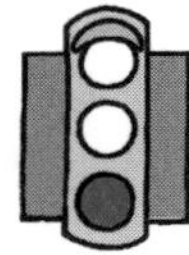

Ready, Set, Go!

You know what I'm going to say here, don't you? *Spend some time together!* Each of you choose something you would really like to do with your spouse (Consider the other's feelings at least a little, okay?), and set aside some time to do it.

CHAPTER SIX

COMMUNICATION

CoMMuNiCATioN

A word aptly spoken is

like apples of gold in

settings of silver.

Proverbs 25:11

The happiest couples are those who spell "us" with a capital "you."

Klaire Provine

Having a **hole** in the head doesn't always indicate an open mind.

I thought talk was **cheap** until I saw our telephone bill.

Happiness is being **married** to your best friend.

—Barbara Weeks

Silence Isn't Always Golden

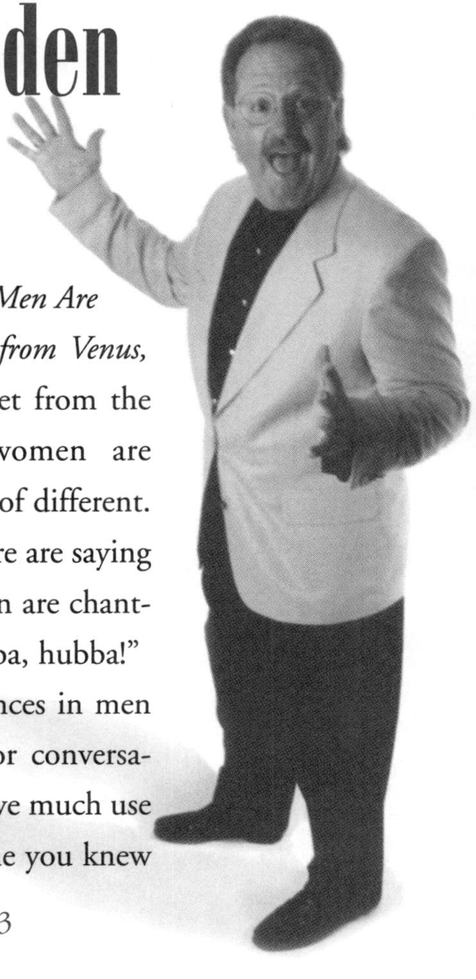

You've heard of the book *Men Are from Mars and Women Are from Venus,* haven't you? The gist you get from the title is that men and women are *different*—worlds apart kind of different. Some of you women out there are saying "Duh!" and some of you men are chanting ol' Swan's mantra, "Hubba, hubba!"

One of the major differences in men and women is their need for conversation. Most men just don't have much use for it. When was the last time you knew of a man who called someone on the phone just to chat? It just doesn't happen! Someone has said that women speak fifty thousand words a day, while men speak only ten thousand. That explains a lot. Business meetings, reports, and employee problems seem to use up all of a man's words by two o'clock in the afternoon. And when he gets home, he's as happy as a pig in a poke sitting in his easy chair, in charge of the channel changer.

On the other hand, most women have plenty of words left over when they get home from work. She, too, may have been involved in just as many meetings, reports, and employee problems during the day, but, hey, she's got lots of words left for an evening visit with her number one guy! And the woman who stays home during the day with no one but children to talk to *really* has some extra words!

So, after work, the scene may go something like this: Husband comes home and heads straight for the easy chair, desiring some peace and quiet—*a little therapy*, he tells himself. Wife comes home, begins supper, tends to the kids, and starts a load of laundry. Then she goes over to him and says, "How was your day, honey? Open your heart to mine."

Being the perceptive guy he is, he thinks, "Oh, no, she's been to another women's conference. Please, don't make me listen to another tape!"

Well, the truth of the matter is, while he may not think he needs it, communication is essential to a great marriage. And yes, there are tons of ways to communicate. A man tends to think that bringing home a paycheck communicates all that needs to be said about his love for his family. And his hard work does speak volumes about his love, as does his wife's. But, right now, I'm talking about *verbal* communication and its value to a relationship. I've dealt with folks from all over the South, and sometimes those hard-headed men tell me, "I told her I loved her when I married her. If I ever change my mind, I'll let her know." Listen, guys, that's just not going to get it.

Once, when I was going to be out of town over Valentine's Day, I wanted to express to Lauree my deep love for her. Being the cultured man that I am, I decided to put thousands of sticky notes all over the house. I put one in the freezer that read, "It may be cold in here, but my heart burns for you, baby." I put another on her pillow that said, "Wish I were here." Oh, sticky notes were everywhere: under the bed, in the cabinets, in the drawers, on the mirrors. I did it up right.

I couldn't wait to hear her words of praise and thanksgiving! So, the minute I got to the hotel, I called. "Lauree, did you get my notes? Weren't they nice? What'd you think?"

"Well, dear, they left sticky stuff all over the house."

You see, Lauree is in the minority of women who don't use many words. And I am one of those rare male birds who loves to talk. I think our word-quotas got somehow mixed up at birth. But God put Lauree and me together so ol' Swan could have someone to share his abundance of words with. Well, after she cleaned off the sticky stuff, she did appreciate my efforts.

You see, no relationship grows without communication. Sharing expressions of love, personal experiences, and lifelong dreams are the "fuel" needed to create an atmosphere for growing closer as the years fly by.

Now, communication is a two-way street: There's the *talking* lane, and there's the *listening* lane. The Bible even tells us to be "quick to listen." But I don't want any of you out there abusing this verse: "Hey, here's a verse that says I don't have to talk. I can just listen. I'm really good at that." Sorry to disappoint you, but that verse does not mean it's okay not to talk to your spouse. Instead, it affirms the value of listening before speaking.

Husbands, if you want to better understand your wife, listen to her. Listen to what she communicates by what she *says*, by what she *doesn't* say, and by what she communicates through her *actions*. Man, that's a tough assignment. I know it's hard. But it's worth the effort. Let her know that you take her seriously and respect what she's saying and feeling. Don't just say something stupid like, "Well, baby, them sure were words!"

Sometimes you gotta pay special attention to hear what she's *not* saying. I know when Laurie's having a bad day by what she doesn't say. I'll call home and say, "Hey, honey love. How are you doing?"

"Okay," she says.

"Is everything all right?"

"Well, I'm doing the best I can."

Now, I'm not a really bright fellow, but I know what's happening at home by reading between the lines. I've trained myself to listen to what Lauree says and to what she doesn't say.

And women, you especially need to listen when a man talks. It may not happen often. A man is not as likely to reveal his heart as quickly as a woman. When he does talk, if his efforts are not handled with care, he will shut up tighter than a drum and may not try again. And listen to what he's not saying. Just like you, men send out nonverbal signals. The key is to make a conscious effort to stay tuned in to your husband's frequency.

If you're a little out of practice in the communication department, start small. You may need to back up and start over with simple topics like you discussed when you were dating. Remember those deep discussions you had way back when: "What is your favorite movie?" or "Who was your favorite teacher?" You'll be surprised how natural and spontaneous your conversation will soon become. When your spouse knows that you care about what he or she thinks and feels, communication walls will come down. Your marriage will grow stronger and your love tank will soon be overflowing.

Fill up on the Word— 1 Corinthians 13

Effective, loving communicators have a lot to learn from the Love Chapter. Almost every verse in this beautiful passage could apply to communication, but we'll focus on just a few phrases: "Love is *patient*, love is *kind* . . . it is *not easily angered* . . . but *rejoices with the truth.*" Sometimes, meaningful communication is downright hard, and it requires real patience to listen and listen again until you understand, to explain and explain again until you are understood. But this is the price love pays.

And truly helpful communication is *kind* and *not easily angered.* How often do our efforts at communication degenerate into shouting matches filled with angry, unkind words? Loving as Christ would have us love is not an easy task. And how important it is that we *rejoice in the truth* when we get down to nitty-gritty honesty. When you hear an honest complaint against you or a truthful confession of wrong, it's not always easy to *rejoice,* but this is what Paul tells us to do.

CHECK YOUR GAUGE

1. Who in your marriage is more talkative, you or your spouse?
2. What typically happens in your relationship

when one of you wants to "talk"? Are you both willing and receptive, or do one or both of you cringe at the thought?

3. What are you better at—listening or talking? How can you improve in your weaker area?
4. What nonverbal clues does your spouse give off that communicate his or her thoughts and feelings? How receptive are you to that sort of communication? What can you do to improve your receptivity?

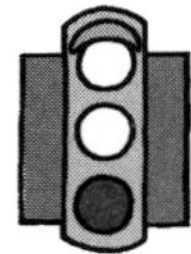

READY, SET, GO!

Put out extra effort this week to verbalize your love for your spouse. Keep doing it until it becomes a regular habit. If it's been a while since you really talked, make a date for a quiet dinner somewhere and plan to talk about something important to you. Be sure to take turns.

7 CHAPTER SEVEN

SUPPORT

Support

For even the Son of Man

did not come to be served,

but to serve, and to give

his life as a ransom for

many.

Mark 10:45

If I am inconsiderate about the comfort of others, or their feelings, or even their little weaknesses; if I am careless about their little hurts and miss opportunities to smooth their way; if I make the sweet running of household wheels more difficult to accomplish, then I know nothing of Calvary's love.

Amy Carmichael

Wishes won't wash **dishes.**

If you do housework for $150 a week, that's domestic service. If you do it for nothing—**that's matrimony.**

Thanks, but We Have a Dishwasher

Some people are just born hospitable. My wife is one of those people. She loves to have people over. She fixes up the house and makes sure everything is just so. Well, one Easter, she invited her whole family over for the big Easter Sunday lunch and egg hunt.

Now, you may or may not be aware that there are different levels of meals. You have your paper-plate meals, you have your everyday meals, and you have your good-china meals. Easter lunch definitely falls in the good-china category.

Lauree spent hours laying out the design of the table. For Lauree, hospitality is an art form! There was some sort of loop de lou out of fabric and lots of candles. Then right in the middle of the table was this gargantuan centerpiece. We were halfway through the meal before I knew my brother-in-law Rick was sitting across from me! I have to admit, though, it really was pretty. She even had those little rings that hold your napkin. And I don't mean paper napkins; I mean the kind you have to wash and iron later.

After lunch, everyone kind of hangs around —you know, forever and ever, amen. The men sleep; the women talk about shopping. Before you know it, it's time for supper. "Just a light snack," someone suggests. Now a light snack is in the "everyday meal" category, so we have to switch from the good china to the pottery. I hear such carrying-ons as, "Your pottery is so nice!

Where did you get it? What pattern is this?" Meanwhile, I'm looking over at the sink where the china dishes are neatly piled up, needing to be washed, and I visualize the pottery dishes piled up beside them. Of course, my sweet baby has to get out a whole new set of forks and knives. "Why can't we just lick the ones we used for lunch?" I want to ask.

"Anyone ready for dessert?" Lauree says, after the pottery is stacked up for washing. I'm thinking, "Yes, the next level—paper plates." She's thinking, "It's Easter—the little china plates would be nice." The day finally draws to an end, and everyone is getting ready to leave. I finally hear her sweet mamma, Kathy, utter the wonderful, melodious words I'd been longing to hear, "Lauree, do you want us to help you with the dishes?"

I'm silently screaming, "Yes, yes, yes!" But you know what Lauree says, don't you? "Oh, don't worry about it. We'll take care of it. We've got a dishwasher." "We've got a dishwasher!" What kind of answer it that? The truth is, it takes a lot of work to get three sets of dishes ready to go in the dishwasher. What about the pots and pans that won't go in the dishwasher? Who's going to do those? I'll tell you who did those. Ol' Swan and his sweet, hospitable wife were up until one in the morning cleaning and putting dishes away.

And I was trying to do it right, trying to put things in the right cabinet—I really was. But after a few minutes of clueless guessing, Lauree speaks up, "Honey, it doesn't go there." I try again. "No, it doesn't go there either." And then the dreaded words: "If you helped me more often, you'd know where it goes." She was right.

Lauree is one of those special folks who loves to serve and open their homes to guests. It's how she says "I love you" to special friends and family. It's the fuel she uses to fill others' love tanks.

Your spouse may have that gift. Chances are

he or she has some gift, maybe several. Whatever they are, you must learn to help your spouse exercise those gifts. Now you may be thinking, "But it's her gift (or his gift), not mine!" Yes, that's true. But here's the thing. If you are one with your partner, then your partner's gifts must become a part of you.

If your wife's gift is hospitality, then hospitality becomes one of your gifts. Kinda scary, huh? If a husband loves his wife, he will serve her. He will not sit in his easy chair, expecting her to be his servant. He will not think through a list of things she should do for him. "Has she ironed my shirts? Has she cooked the supper? Where are my socks? Is the bed made?" Instead, he will be creative in finding ways to serve her. He will be sensitive to what must be done to "run the household," and he will find ways to participate. He will want to ease her load because he loves her and wants the best for her.

Similarly, a wife who loves her husband

Support

doesn't demand her "rights." She doesn't try to think up jobs she can dump on her husband. She doesn't whine about what she has or doesn't have. Instead, she thoughtfully seeks ways to serve her husband. And she participates in and supports his gifts.

You see, when both spouses operate under this principle, the food will get cooked, the dishes done, the socks found, and the beds made out of love for each other and a desire to serve one another. There will be no power struggle to see who can hold out the longest, forcing the other to do the chore. When you and your spouse support each other, you communicate this message: "You are a person of worth and dignity. You have much to contribute to others and I want to help." God wants this fuel in your marriage.

Fill Up on the Word—1 Corinthians 13

When you think about it, your spouse's gifts are from *God*. When you support and help your husband or wife use these God-given gifts, you are cooperating with God. If you thwart your mate's gifts, you hinder God's work. That's a pretty sobering thought, isn't it?

First Corinthians 13 speaks volumes about being supportive and helpful to the ones we love: "Love . . . is *not self-seeking*. . . . It always *protects*." True love means seeking the interests of another. It means *protecting* the gifts God gave them by nurturing and supporting and helping those gifts grow.

Check Your Gauge

1. What is your spouse particularly good at? In other words, what are your spouse's God-given gifts?
2. Do you currently cooperate with God in supporting your spouse's gifts, or do you hinder his work? Specifically, how do you cooperate; how do you hinder?
3. What specific things can you do to nurture and encourage your mate's gifts?
4. What is a power struggle? Think of a specific time when you sought to gain the upper hand? How could you handle that situation differently?

Ready, Set, Go!

As husband and wife, sit down together and talk about each other's gifts. Take turns talking about how you can use your own gifts for the Lord and how your spouse can support you in the use of your gifts. Then tell each other what you appreciate about the other's gifts and ways you plan to support them.

8

CHAPTER EIGHT

EXPRESSING LOVE

Expressing Love

Let no debt remain outstanding, except the continuing debt to love one another.

Romans 13:8

You will find as you look back upon your life that the moments when you have really lived are the moments when you have done things in the spirit of love.

Henry Drummond

Happiness is an **inside** job.

—William A. Ward

Anybody can be a **heart specialist.** The only requirement is loving somebody.

—Angie Papadakis

How 'bout Them Cowboys

Art Linkletter became famous for his interaction with children. For years he had a popular television show featuring children expressing their views on all kinds of topics, and he later compiled a book titled *Kids Say the Darndest Things.* Art Linkletter reminded us old folks that many of life's most valuable principles are taught by our children—if we'll just be open and flexible.

Jesus tells us in Matthew 18 that we must *become like little children* if we want to enter the kingdom of heaven. He goes on to say, "The greatest person in the kingdom of heaven is the one who makes himself humble like a child." Children can be our greatest resource. I'm so thankful for my two boys, Chad and Dusty, and what they've already taught me in the short years we have had together. No telling what I'll learn from them in the years to come!

A few years back I was pastoring at the First Baptist Church in West Monroe, Louisiana, when my oldest son, Chad, took it upon himself to teach old dad a lesson in expressing love. Now, I'm a pretty affectionate guy. I thought I knew and practiced just about every expression of love. I love to hug and kiss, I write notes, and I say sweet things to my family. I love to hold hands with my honey love. I squeeze her hand three times and that tells her, "I love you," and she squeezes mine back twice. She's asking, "How much?" That's our playful way of expressing our love for each other.

And I love to hug and kiss on my boys too. No, I don't do it in public—I know better than to embarrass them. But, at home, I hug on them often. But one night, when I went into Chad's room to tell him good-night and hug and kiss him, he stopped me short. "Dad, we're men," he said.

"Son, I'm your daddy," I said.

"But Dad, we're men."

I tried to explain to him how my dad's culture had such a hard time being outwardly affectionate and how I'd always wanted that growing up. The limit of my dad's world was too often a handshake—even for a small boy! Even now, when I hug ol' Floyd Leon, he doesn't know how to handle it. Although he's getting better, he'll just say something like, "You all drive carefully now. You were good kids. We never had to bail you out of jail or anything like that. You all be careful." Oh, we knew he loved us. Hugging was just hard for his generation.

"Chad," I said, "I always wanted it to be different with my boys. I wanted to be able to . . ."

Chad finally interrupted me, "We could do what they do on *Home Improvement.*"

Well, who's to say we can't learn from a television show. So I said, "Okay, son, what do they do?"

Chad explained that the father and his three sons had a special code way of saying I love you. That way, whenever they were in public, they could use their code words. "They say, 'How 'bout them Detroit Tigers?' and that means 'I love you,' " he explained.

And he had a plan all figured out for us—I could tell he'd been thinking about it for a while. We could say, "How 'bout them Cowboys?"

Chad saw my reluctance, "C'mon, Dad . . ."

And I said, "C'mon, son . . ."

Still not convinced, but because I love my son, I finally said, "Hey, Chad, how 'bout them Cowboys?"

He smiled a big grin and said, "Yeah."

Feeling like all fathers do when they witness their children crossing a milestone that painfully reminds them of how fast they grow, I sadly returned to our bedroom. I told Lauree all about it. But she wasn't alarmed.

"It's okay, honey, he's just going through a stage. You just keep loving him. It'll all work out, just wait and see."

A week later, after much begging and pleading from my family, I decided to take them to a country-western concert. Now this was a sacrifice trip for me—for two very good reasons. The number one reason was the singer was George Strait. Now, my wife thinks George Strait is about the cutest thing in this world. I asked her what he has that I don't and she said, "A lot." I decided to let it go at that. The number two reason was it was in Shreveport. That was a 180-mile round-trip for me on a Saturday night when I had to preach two sermons the next morning. You see what a sacrifice this was for me?

Anyway, we got all duded up. Chad and I had on our Mo Better shirts. Little Dusty had on a Brooks and Dunn shirt with flames of fire on it. And Lauree, well she looked more like Lori Morgan. She didn't look like a pastor's wife, if you know what I mean; she looked more like a deacon's wife. I must admit, we were all *lookin' good*. We piled into the Surburban and headed for Shreveport.

When George came out on stage, the crowd went wild. Lauree and the boys were singing along, clapping, and yelling. I was silently adding up the time it would take us to get home. Counting bathroom stops, I figured we wouldn't get home till 1:30 A.M. I was feeling more sorry for myself by the minute.

About that time, Chad worked his way over to where I was standing. He put his arm around me and with a big grin on his face said, "Hey,

Dad. How 'bout them Cowboys?" That's all it took. Man, I was into the concert. I was singing. I was clapping. We all took our picture with the cardboard cutout of George Strait. We bought the cassette tape, and we sang George Strait songs all the way home. It was the best concert I have ever been to because of four simple words: "How 'bout them Cowboys?"

The next morning, as the church was singing hymns, I was humming, "All My Exes Live in Texas." My kid, my boy, my son had taught me a lesson. He taught me that there's all kinds of ways to fill our love tanks, just as long as we keep filling.

Fill up on the Word—1 Corinthians 13

Paul's summary words in his timeless description of love say it all: Love "always *protects,* always *trusts,* always *hopes,* always *perseveres."* One of the most important traits of love is the *always* part. Love always . . . As parents, we naturally want to protect our children, but we need to have that same feeling toward our life-mates. I'm not speaking only of physical protection, but protection of fragile egos and breakable hearts. I'm talking of protecting our mate's reputation by always speaking well of each other in public and by gently demanding that others respect them too. Love always hopes and always trusts. It looks to the future with optimistic belief that love will endure. It trusts the heart and motives of the loved one so much that it gives a little slack when our mates don't behave perfectly.

And finally, love always perseveres. Love is work. I know that's not the way the movies make it out to be, but it's the truth. Loving, lasting relationships require perseverance and hard work. Keep after it, Paul says, for love *always* . . .

CHECK YOUR GAUGE

1. What's the most precious lesson about expressing love that you've learned from a child?
2. Do you have a difficult time being affectionate like my dad, Floyd Leon? If so, do you think your loved ones want more affection

from you? What small steps can you take right now to begin expressing your love more?

3. Think of each family member. What expressions of love would be meaningful to each one?
4. What about the 1 Corinthians instructions on love are the most difficult for you? What are the easiest?

Ready, Set, Go!

Gather your whole family together for a "love tank" session. Ask each member to tell what expressions of love "fill their tanks." You go first to get everyone started.

PRODUCTS TO BRING MERRIMENT TO YOUR SOUL

Dennis Swanberg enjoys serving as America's Minister of Encouragement! Dr. Swanberg's products (videos/audios/books, etc.) can be ordered through Lasting Impressions.

Video/audio

Back to Back with Laughter
Loosen up, Laugh, and Live
Laughter from the Rafters
Is Your Love Tank Full?
Everlasting Laughter

Book

Is Your Love Tank Full?

Swan's Lasting Impressions
318-397-8745
318-397-8743 fax
PO Box 1495
West Monroe, LA 71294

SCHEDULE "THE SWAN" FOR YOUR SPECIAL EVENT

Dr. Swanberg enjoys hosting conferences, banquets, and other special events for churches, schools, and businesses. The Swan knows how to instill hope and success in the lives of others with his unusual wit and wisdom. His fascinating impersonations, down-home stories, and inspirational "merry heart" doeth good like a medicine to all who hear him. Schedule "The Swan" today for your group.

Swan's Lasting Impressions
318-397-8745
318-397-8743 fax
PO Box 1495
West Monroe, LA 71294